# HOW PEOPLE LIVE

# FAMILIES AROUND THE WORLD

## JENNY VAUGHAN

Editorial planning
**Jollands Editions**

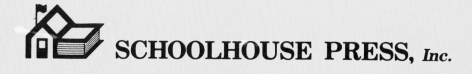

## SCHOOLHOUSE PRESS, Inc.

Copyright © 1986 by Schoolhouse Press, Inc.
191 Spring Street, Lexington,
Massachussetts 02173-8087
ISBN 0-8086-1067-8 (hardback)
ISBN 0-8086-1055-4 (paperback)

Original copyright, © Macmillan Education Limited 1986
© BLA Publishing Limited 1986

Designed and produced by BLA Publishing Limited,
Swan Court, East Grinstead, Sussex, England.
*Also in* LONDON · HONG KONG · TAIPEI · SINGAPORE · NEW YORK
**A Ling Kee Company**

Color origination by Planway Ltd
Printed and bound in Spain by
Gráficas Estella, S. A. Navarra.

86/87/88/89          6  5  4  3  2  1

## Acknowledgements
The Publishers wish to thank the following
organizations for their invaluable assistance in the
preparation of this book.

Kuwait Embassy
NASA
Oxfam
Shell

## Photographic credits
*t = top b = bottom l = left r = right*

**cover:** Anthony Bannister/NHPA

4 ZEFA; 5*t* The Hutchison Library; 5*b* ZEFA;
6 Anthony Bannister/NHPA; 6/7 Brian Hawkes/NHPA;
7 Patrick Fagot/NHPA; 8 ZEFA; 9*t* Chris Fairclough;
9*b*, 10, 11 The Hutchison Library; 12 ZEFA; 13*t*, 13*b*,
14*t*, 14*b* The Hutchison Library; 15 Shell; 16 The
Hutchison Library; 17*t* South American Pictures;
17*b* ZEFA; 18 South American Pictures; 19*l* ZEFA;
19*r* The Hutchison Library; 20 ZEFA; 21*t* The
Hutchison Library; 21*b* Macmillan Education; 22, 23*t*,
23*b*, 24*t*, 24*b*, 25 ZEFA; 26*t*, 26*b*, 27 The Hutchison
Library; 28 Chris Fairclough; 29*t* Douglas Dickens;
29*b* ZEFA; 30 Douglas Dickens; 31, 32, 33*t*, 33*b*, 34 The
Hutchison Library; 35*t*, 36*b* ZEFA; 36 The Hutchison
Library; 37*t* Kuwait Embassy; 37*b*, 38, 39*t*, 39*b* The
Hutchison Library; 40, 41*t* ZEFA; 41*b*, 42/43 The
Hutchison Library; 43 Oxfam; 44/45 NASA

**Note to the reader**
In this book there are some words in the text which are printed in **bold** type. This shows that the
word is listed in the glossary on page 46. The glossary gives a brief explanation of words which may
be new to you.

# Contents

# Introduction

A family is a group of people who are related to each other. Our closest family consists of the **relatives** with whom we live and grow up. Some families are small. Others can be very large. No two families are the same.

▼ Sometimes children work with their parents. This girl is helping her father to sell oranges in the market in Varanasi, India.

Most people live in some kind of family. Perhaps you live with your mother and father. You may have brothers and sisters. All these people make up your family. People who have lost their parents, or who have only one parent, enjoy family life with other relatives.

This book is about families around the world. Many families living in one place form a group called a **community**. This book is about communities as well as about families.

## Staying Together

It was not easy to travel far from home before there were cars and trains. People stayed in one place. Families worked together on the land and in the home. They had to work together in order to grow enough food to feed themselves. When the children grew up, they did not move far from home. They usually married people from the community. People who lived in the same village were often related to each other.

Today, people move around more than they used to. Some young people may move into a nearby city to work. Other people may look for work in another part of the country, or overseas.

## Settling Down

Families change all the time. As sons and daughters grow older, they leave home. They want a home of their own. Many young people have children and start new families. When a man and woman get married, they become part of each other's family as well as their own.

Some people have large families with many children. Others choose to have one or two children. Many people do not marry. They may choose to live alone or to live with friends. Everyone has relatives even if they do not live with them. We are all part of a family.

◀ This family lives on the Ivory Coast in West Africa. It will soon be bedtime for the small boy.

▼ It is vacation time for this family. They are on a beach in Majorca, a Spanish island in the Mediterranean. They can swim together in the sea. The children will enjoy playing in the sand.

# Animals and Their Families

Animals do not think about staying alive or about having young. They know they must try to stay alive and produce more young animals. They are acting by **instinct**. In this way, each kind of animal, or **species**, will go on living. It will **survive**.

Insects lay hundreds of eggs, and then they leave them. They do not look after them at all. Female butterflies lay their eggs on a leaf or a twig. The eggs hatch into caterpillars. Animals and birds will eat most of them. A few will survive because so many eggs were laid.

A caterpillar will take nearly a year to grow. Then, it makes a hard skin around itself. The skin is called a **chrysalis**. Inside the skin, the caterpillar grows into a butterfly. The butterfly breaks the skin and crawls out. Because most butterflies live for only about a week, the females lay their eggs very quickly. These stages in a butterfly's life are called its **life cycle**.

## Bird Families

Birds care for their young like many other animals. They look after them until they can survive on their own.

A male and female swan will stay together all their lives. They build their nest in the same place each year. The female lays about six eggs. She sits on them to keep them warm and to protect them from attack. Sometimes, the male swan sits on them, too.

The eggs hatch after about five weeks. The young swans, or **cygnets**, are soon in the water. They follow their mother everywhere. The mother protects the cygnets and leads them to food. They are learning how to survive. After five months, they can look after themselves.

◄ **This African moon moth is laying eggs. When it has finished, it will fly away and leave the eggs.**

Other kinds of birds do not pair for life. They find new mates each year. They stay together until the new family of young birds can fly.

## Mammals

Animals which give birth to live young are called **mammals**. Mammals do not lay eggs. Human beings are mammals. One of the animals most like human beings is the chimpanzee.

A female chimp has one baby at a time. The young chimp stays with its mother until it is about six years old. It learns from her and from other chimps in the group. Some chimpanzees stay alive until they are 40 years old or more.

Chimps live in Africa in large family groups. They are friendly animals. They sometimes greet each other with a hug. They clean each other's fur for a long time each day. This is called **grooming**.

▲ Swans look after their cygnets while the cygnets are small. When the cygnets grow bigger, they will leave their parents. They will look after themselves.

▶ Monkeys spend a lot of time getting rid of insects from each other's fur. It is part of the monkey's family life.

# Human Families

▼ It is playtime in the park for these two children and their mother.

Human families around the world vary in size. Some are small. Others are large. Over the years, the size of a family can change. A small family can get bigger because someone gets married. This brings new relatives into the family. In each large family group, there are smaller groups.

## Small Families

The simplest family group is made up of one parent or relative and a child. Many people grow up in this type of family. One of the parents might have died, or perhaps the parents do not live together any more. They may be **divorced**. If the parents are divorced, perhaps the child or children will live with their mother. If she marries again, her new husband is their stepfather. If they live with their father and he remarries, they will have a stepmother. The stepparent's children will become their stepbrothers and stepsisters.

Children sometimes have to live away from their parents. Then, children may live with another family for a time. The parents in this other family will become their **foster** parents.

Some children might become part of a new family. For some reason, their own parents cannot take care of them. The children may be taken care of, or **adopted**, by new parents.

## Other Relatives

Each small family is part of a larger one. Your grandparents are your closest relatives after your parents, sisters, and brothers. Uncles and aunts are also close relatives. These are your parents' brothers and sisters, and their wives and husbands. Their children are your cousins. All of these people are related to you by birth or by marriage. They are all members of the family.

When people marry, they bring other people into the family. If your sister marries, her husband will be your brother-in-law. If you marry, you may have a father-in-law and a mother-in-law. They are the parents of your wife or husband.

Some people do not see their relatives very often. The family may meet only when there is a wedding or a funeral. Other people live and grow up with many of their relatives.

▲ This Japanese family is going shopping. The family enjoys going out together.

▶ These children are at school in Wolverhampton in England. The children all come from the local community.

# Large Families

Some people live and grow up in large family groups, or **households**. You may have friends whose grandparents live with them. In some families, aunts, uncles, and cousins may also live together. There are large families like this in many parts of the world. They are often found where people work on the land. There are plenty of people to share the work on the land and in the home. The whole family can care for the young, the sick, and the old. They might live in the same group of homes, or **compound**, all their lives.

There is less space for large family groups in cities. Households there are much smaller.

## Family Groups

Large families that live together can be run in many ways. The oldest person is often the most important. She or he is the head of the family.

The Ashanti people live in Ghana in northwest Africa. The women work on the land to grow the family's food. An Ashanti woman does not live in the same house as her husband. She lives in her own house with her children. Her children will one day have their own land. It will come from their mother's family, not their father's.

In some Indian families, young men live in their parents' compound. When they marry, their wives and children live there, too. The household can become very large. The grandfather is head of the family.

▼ This family lives in south India. The six children all help in the fields. They all have to work together to grow food to feed the family.

▲ In northern Nigeria, some African men have more than one wife. This man is seen with his five wives and their small children.

## Tribes

Some people belong to family groups called **tribes**. Each person in the tribe is related to all the other people in it. The people who began the family were the **ancestors** of the tribe.

Members of a tribe all come from the same part of a country. They speak the same language. They live in the same way.

Some tribes are very small. They may live in a few villages. Other tribes have millions of people.

## Many Wives and Husbands

Having more than one wife at the same time is called **polygamy**. Many men used to have more than one wife. There were more people to work on the land and in the home. Men who were rich enough to keep many wives and children were important.

Today, polygamy still happens in some countries. The Muslim religion allows a man to have up to four wives. All the wives must be treated in the same way. Most Muslims now choose to have only one wife.

Having more than one husband is called **polyandry**. There are very few places where this still happens. Women in Tibet sometimes marry more than one husband. They might marry several brothers in one family.

# Keeping Alive

Every family is different, but all families need the same things. They all need food, clothes, and somewhere to live. Young children, old people, and sick people need to be taken care of.

## Living off the Land

Some families go from place to place to look for food for their animals. They are **nomads**. Most nomad families live in the deserts of the world.

There are Bedouin families living in the deserts of the Middle East and northwest Africa. They keep sheep, goats, and camels. They live in tents made from the hair of goats and camels. Their animals provide them with meat and milk.

Millions of people in the world are farmers. Many of these farmers can grow just enough crops to feed themselves. They are **subsistence** farmers. Large families in Africa and India often live in this way. They have little land. They have few **machines** to help them. Everyone, including the children, must work hard to grow food.

In a good year, these farmers may grow more crops than they need. This is called a **surplus**. The family can sell the food they do not need. Then, they can buy things they cannot make or grow themselves.

Farmers with more land can grow crops and raise animals to sell. The family still works hard, but they have more money.

Europe, and the USSR often have nurseries. Young children can stay there while their parents are at work.

Some families can choose how to look after their children. One parent can stay at home, or both parents may work part time. They take turns looking after the children.

It is not as easy for some parents or single parents. They may not find anyone to take care of their children. They may not have enough money to pay them. They have to stay at home.

In some countries the **State** gives money to people who cannot find jobs. It also gives a little help to people who are taking care of old or sick relatives at home.

---

◀ This boy lives in northern Pakistan. He spends most of his time helping to take care of the family's goats and sheep. You can see how few plants there are for the animals to eat. The family must move around. They must search for food for the animals.

▼ Most adults in China go out to work. There are nurseries where parents can leave young children while they are at work.

They can pay people to help them. They can buy machines like tractors. Farms in such places as Europe, North America, and Australia can be very large. The farmers can buy all kinds of machines to help with the farm work. All the family may not need to work on the farm.

## Life in the City

People who live in towns and cities cannot grow their food. They must buy the things they need to live. Some people can earn a living from home. Perhaps they make things to sell, or have a store. Other people have to go out to work. They must find a job to earn money.

In many families, all the adults go out to work. The children spend the day at school or in a nursery. **Factories** in China,

# Working Away from Home

Many people work in stores, factories, and offices. Some workers can walk or ride a bike to work. Others live farther away. They have to travel to work by bus, train, or car. People who travel to work every day are called **commuters**.

Most commuters begin work at the same time each day. The roads and trains are very crowded as people travel to work. The times when people travel to and from work are called "rush hours."

Some people work a long way from home. They may have jobs which take them all over the country. They cannot come home each night. The weekend is the only time the family can be together.

▲ This is rush hour in Beijing. Many people go to work on bicycles.

▼ The women in this village in Botswana are building a house. They work together on some jobs. The men leave the village for part of the year in order to look after the cattle.

▶ These men are working on an oil rig off the coast of Scotland. They can earn a lot of money, but they will not see their families very often.

## Moving with the Seasons

Some people work in different places throughout the year. In Botswana, families move when their cattle move. They stay with their cattle in grazing areas called cattle posts. They also have to work on the land near their homes. That is where they grow their own food. The children help on the land when they are not at school.

In northwest Africa, families cannot grow enough crops to sell. Because they need money to buy things for the family, the men go away to work. They spend part of the year away from home. They go to the cities to earn money. The women grow the food and look after the families. The men come home to help with the work on the land.

## Working Abroad

Some people move to other countries to find work. They choose a country where they hope to earn a lot of money.

Many of these people hope to return home as soon as they can. They try to save money. Some plan to buy land or to go into business when they return home. This is not always easy. It may take much longer to save the money than they thought at first. Families may be split up for years.

There are other ways a family can be split up by work. Skilled workers, like engineers and scientists, may be needed in another country. They earn a lot of money, but they may have to move around the world. Their families cannot always travel with them.

# Working at Home

There is always work to do at home. People do not get paid for this work, but it has to be done. Cooking, cleaning, and washing clothes for a family take up a lot of time.

## Running the Home

Working at home can be more than doing the housework. Many of the men of Lesotho in southern Africa work in mines far from their homes. Some men come home only once a year. The women, old people, and children stay behind in the villages. The women of Lesotho work on the land. They also have to take care of their homes and their children because the men are not there to help.

The women grow crops, take care of the animals, and collect firewood and water. Collecting water can take a long time. There are parts of Lesotho where there are no pumps or faucets in the villages. The women may have to walk to a stream or a well. They have to carry the water home in pots or cans. There are many other parts of the world where there is no fresh water close to people's homes.

The children in Lesotho have to work, too. They help in the home and on the land before they go to school. They work in the evenings, too.

▼ This Sudanese woman is grinding grain with a stone to make flour. She wets the flour as she grinds it. This makes a dough for baking bread.

► These women live high up in the Andes Mountains in Peru. The woman on the right is weaving a blanket. She is using wool from her animals. She will sell the blanket in the local market. Her family have earned money from weaving for hundreds of years. The young girl will learn how to make rugs, too.

## Working in the Home

In the past, people like spinners, weavers, blacksmiths, and potters worked in their homes. They used part of their homes as a **workshop**. They made goods, like cloth and pots, for the people in their town or village. Today, many of these jobs are done in factories.

In some places, you will still find people doing this kind of work at home. Sometimes, this is because the way of working has not changed at all. In other places, it is because people want to work in the home. They can arrange their working hours to suit themselves.

Instead of working in an office, some people now do office work at home. They may have a computer which keeps them in touch with the office. In the future, more people may work in the home in this way.

► More and more people now work at home. They use a computer for their work. The computer may be linked to their offices, so they do not need to go to work every day.

# Building Homes

We all need a place where we can sleep and eat, and where we can take shelter from the weather. The weather, or **climate**, is different from one part of the world to another. Some places are hot and dry. Others are hot and wet, or cold and wet, or cold and dry! The weather changes at different times of the year. Houses must be built to suit the climate.

▼ These people live on an island on Lake Titicaca in South America. They make their homes from reeds that grow nearby. Sometimes they use other materials as well. Two of the buildings here have tin roofs.

## Simple Homes

People often make their homes to suit the way they live. Some desert people are nomads. They do not stay in one place for very long. They live in tents which they can fold up easily. When they move, they take their homes with them. The tents are carried on the backs of camels.

People build their homes out of all kinds of things. They use whatever is at hand. Some of these thing are simple **materials**, such as straw and clay. Bricks have been made out of straw and clay for thousands of years.

In Iraq, there are people who live near marshes. **Reeds** grow thick and tall in the marshes. The people build their homes out of these reeds.

Many homes are made with mud or clay. In parts of Africa, people use clay to build the walls of their homes. They use grass for

the roofs. One family may have several small houses. There are separate houses for different members of the family. They are built close together. Today, many people also use building materials like tin sheets for roofs. They last longer than the grass roofs, but they cost money.

▲ Millions of people work in cities. They often live in houses on the edges of the cities. These houses are in Brisbane, Australia.

▼ These buildings in the Middle East have thick mud walls and shutters at the windows. Both help to keep the rooms cool.

## Houses and Apartments

The people who build houses today still use clay to make bricks and roof tiles. They still use wood to make doors and roof frames. These materials which have been used for so long are called **traditional** materials.

Builders also use other things. Sand, small stones, and a kind of clay called cement are mixed together to make **concrete**. Concrete blocks are larger than bricks and are very hard.

Builders can make houses of any shape or size when using these materials. The houses often have several rooms. Each room is used for a different purpose. Sometimes, a young couple will rent or buy a small house or apartment. It may only have one bedroom. When they have children, they look for a bigger place to live.

In towns and cities, there may not be enough land for houses. Apartment buildings are built. These can become crowded, too. It is not easy for a large family to live in a small apartment, but many families do so.

# Homes around the World

In the African grasslands, people have to protect themselves and their homes from wild animals. The Masai people live in Kenya and Tanzania. They live in small, low houses. They build a thick, thorn fence around each group of homes. At night, they bring their cattle inside this fence. They do this so that lions and leopards cannot attack the cattle.

Insects are another danger. Flies and mosquitoes carry diseases. People try to keep them out of their homes. They put screens across the windows. This lets in the air but keeps out the insects. People who live near rivers sometimes build their homes above the ground on poles called **stilts**. They do this in Vietnam and Kampuchea. When there is a flood, the homes are safe from the water.

## Sharing with Others

People live in villages in many parts of the world. The families share many things. There may be just one faucet or a well which everyone uses. Sometimes, families share machines for working the land. They work on the land together. By sharing things, all the people in the village know each other.

People who live in cities often share things, too. They share the same parks. Their garbage cans are emptied by the same city workers. If they live in an apartment house, they will probably share a superintendent. This person will take care of the inside of the building.

◄ This is Rio Hondo. It is a fishing village in the Philippines. The homes are built on stilts to protect them from floods.

▲ The most important crop in this village in Tanzania is corn. The woman is getting the corncobs ready for storing. The cobs are left to dry on the raised platform. When they are dry, the cobs will be stored.

## Machines in the Home

Machines can make life easier in the home. In cold countries, houses need to be heated. In a cold climate, it is more comfortable to have warm rooms and hot water. In some hot climates, houses need to be kept cool. A machine called an **air conditioner** does this. It keeps all the rooms cool in very hot weather.

There are refrigerators and stoves to help people to store and cook food. There are washing machines and machines for drying wet clothes. Radios and televisions tell us what is going on in the world. We can talk to our family or our friends on the telephone.

▲ Making pancakes is fun! This family has all kinds of machines to help with the work in the home. How many different machines can you see in the picture?

# Religious Beliefs

Many people in the world believe in a god or many gods. Religions are ideas about God and how the world was made. They make us think about how to live our lives. Religious beliefs are often alike. They usually teach that we should care for each other.

Hinduism is the main religion of India. Hindus believe that they will live again in another life after they die. They have many gods and goddesses. Hindus believe that life is a gift and that they should not harm any living thing. Buddhists believe this, too. There are many Buddhists in Southeast Asia.

Followers of Judaism, Christianity, and Islam believe in only one God. Judaism is the religion of the Jewish people. Christianity grew out of Judaism. Its founder was Jesus Christ. Christians believe that Jesus is the son of God. Both Judaism and Christianity teach people to be kind to their neighbors. Most other religions teach this, too.

Islam is the main religion in the Middle East, North Africa, and parts of Asia. It was founded by a man called Muhammad. Followers of Islam are called Muslims.

## Everyday Life

When people follow a religion, it is part of their everyday life. Muslims pray five times a day even when they are at work.

Nearly every Hindu family has a place in the home where they pray. They may have a statue of a god or goddess. Each morning, everyone in the family will pray there.

Some religions have a day for prayer. For Muslims, it is Friday. Christians go to church on Sundays. For Jewish people, the Sabbath is a day for the family to be together. It begins with a special meal on Friday night. On Saturday, the family worships at the **synagogue**.

◄ This man has stopped in the desert to pray. Muslims pray five times a day. They always pray facing their holy city of Mecca.

# Forbidden Food

Many religions have rules about what people may or may not eat. Hindus, for example, do not eat beef. This is because they believe that the cow is **holy**.

Jews have many rules about food. They do not eat pork or shellfish. They do not eat meat and milk in the same meal. Their food has to be made in a special way, called *kosher*. In the Hebrew language, this word means "right."

Muslims do not eat pork or drink alcohol. The name for food that Muslims are allowed to eat is *halal*, which means "lawful."

Some religions have their own holy books. *The Koran* tells Muslims how to live and what to believe. Jews and Christians read the *Bible*. Sikhs read the *Guru Granth Sahib*.

▼ The cow is a sacred animal to Hindus. Nobody would try to move this cow in the streets of Varanasi. Hindus come to Varanasi from all parts of India to bathe in the holy Ganges River.

▲ The Sabbath is a time for Jewish families to be together. This family is starting its Friday evening meal on the eve of the Sabbath. The father is blessing the Sabbath wine.

# Weddings

Weddings mark the start of a marriage. They are the way that a man and woman tell people that they want to live together and care for each other. The families of the woman and the man come to the wedding. They wish the bride and bridegroom well. They give them presents to help them set up a new home.

Weddings can be held in many different ways. Every religion has its own wedding customs. At a wedding, the bride and groom are telling their families and friends that now they are a new family. They say they will try to live in the way their religion tells them to live. They write this down, too.

Perhaps the bride and groom have no religion. They may have another kind of wedding. This is called a **civil** wedding. It

means that they have said they will live together and be a family. The laws of the country will then say that they are married.

## Laws about Marriage

Most countries have laws about marriage. You cannot marry close relatives like your brother or sister. You cannot marry at all until you are the age the country allows. In many countries, the law says that your wife or husband is now your closest relative. If you die, everything you have will belong to her or him. When you both die, your property will be given to your children.

◀ The bride and groom at this wedding in Japan are wearing traditional clothes. They are both wearing special wedding kimonos. The other men wear suits.

◄ This young Russian couple have just got married. All weddings in the USSR are civil with no religious ceremony. Most Russian brides wear the traditional white dress.

► A Hindu wedding. The bride wears a fine silk sari and a lot of jewelry. There are flowers everywhere. A wedding meal is ready. It is a time of great importance for the two families.

## Choosing a Partner

Most people expect to choose the person they will marry. In some parts of the world, young men and women do not choose a partner. Parents look for husbands and wives for their children. This is called an **arranged marriage**.

There are still many arranged marriages in Japan, China, and India. The couple getting married may hardly know each other. Their parents have agreed to the marriage for their children. Sometimes, the parents still use a **matchmaker** to help

them. A matchmaker is someone who finds the right marriage partners for people.

In Europe, marriages used to be arranged because families wanted more land or money. The bride brought land, goods, or money to her husband's family. This was her **dowry**. Dowries are still given in some parts of the world. A bride's family may pay for the wedding meal.

All these weddings are times when the families get together. After the wedding is over, most people have a party. Everyone is happy to welcome a new family.

# Family Celebrations

There are times when all the family come together. A wedding is one of these times. A birthday is another. The day when we were born is a special day for us. We remember it every year. Our families remember our birthday, too. They may give us presents or money.

## Young Children

For Christian families, there is a special time when a child becomes a member of the Church. At that time the child is given a Christian name. A christening is a naming **ceremony**. They are always family occasions.

Hindus hold a head-shaving ceremony. This happens when the child is about one year old. A priest and a barber come to the house. The child's hair is shaved and prayers are said. The parents of the child then give candy to their family and friends.

▲ This family is very happy. It is their son's first birthday. Birthday cakes are usually decorated with one candle for each year of a person's life.

◄ Christmas celebrates the birth of Jesus Christ. This family lives in London. They are opening their presents in front of a Christmas tree.

▲ A Jewish boy is reading from the holy writings of Judaism called the *Torah*. He will soon come of age. It will be his *Bar Mitzvah*.

## Growing Up

When children grow up, we say they "come of age." We do not think that they are children any more.

A *Bar Mitzvah* happens on the Sabbath after a Jewish boy's thirteenth birthday. The Bar Mitzvah boy reads to his family and friends from the Jewish holy writings. He is then blessed by a **rabbi**. Then, he can take part in the life of the religious community. He is a grown-up person. There is the same sort of ceremony for Jewish girls. This is called a *Bat Mitzvah*.

There are different coming-of-age ceremonies all over the world. When **Aborigine** boys in Australia are about to become adults, they leave their families. They go into the desert by themselves for a few days. They have nothing to eat. The adults they have left behind sing songs and do special dances. When the children come home, their families say they are now grown up. They are not children.

In many countries, the law says that people are grown up when they are 18 years old. Then, they can take part in choosing the country's leaders. They can **vote** in the elections. They can leave home if they want to. Most people have a party when they "come of age."

## Growing Old

Old people have many things to **celebrate**. They may have been married for a long time. Some people have been married for 50 years. This is called their "golden" wedding anniversary. All the family celebrates with them. Other people have lived for a very long time, and their birthdays are very special. Old people can teach the family and the community many things about how to live their lives.

# The Wider Family

▼ This family lives on the island of Celebes in Indonesia. Most of the families in the village community earn their living from fishing.

Most families live near other people. The word "community" can mean people who live in a small village. It can also mean the people in a part of a large town or city.

People who live near each other may share many things. They may speak the same language and have the same customs. They may share ideas about how their community should be run. A community can be like a large family.

## Village Life

A village is a community. In many villages, people do the same kinds of work. This could be mining for coal, or it could be fishing or farming. When people live and work together, they get to know each other well. Many of them may be related to one another.

In a village community, people share many things. The children play together. Older people may meet in cafés or clubs. People share hard times, too. In a fishing village, the whole community suffers when a boat sinks at sea. A mining village suffers when there is an accident down in the mine. If the mine closes down or the fishing is stopped, most of the village people may be out of work.

Today, many people leave their villages to look for work in the cities. New people are moving into the villages. They may work in the cities and travel there each day. They may spend most of their time away from the village. They may not want to join in village life. Then, it is more difficult for the village to be a community.

## City Life

A town or city may be made up of many small communities. People in a street or a **neighborhood** may feel that they are a community. Like villagers, they may share the same stores and schools. They may work with each other.

In some cities, there are people whose families have come from other parts of the world. They often live near each other. This helps them to feel less like strangers in the city. People in the neighborhood may speak the same language and share the same religion. They build up their own community, and they are also part of city life.

Communities like these are important to a city. They bring to the whole city new ideas about food, music, art, and many other things. They make the city a more interesting place.

▲ It is market day in Aix-en-Provence in France. People come to the market once a week to buy food. They also come to meet friends. Markets like this help to keep a community together.

► There are Chinese communities in many of the world's large cities. This is San Francisco's Chinatown.

# Living in Groups

## A Village in India

Village life in some parts of India has not changed much over many years. The people try to agree about how the community should be run. They share the same religion and the same ideas about the way they live. They agree about family life and how children should be brought up.

Older people are very important in the village. They have lived for a long time in the village. They can help people to decide what to do. Perhaps two people want the same piece of land. They cannot agree about who owns the land or who should grow crops on it. The older people may remember who owned the land first. The younger people ask the older ones to help them to decide.

When a group of people live together, they try to agree about the way they will live. They make rules about what to do and what not to do. Most rules in a family are about being kind and helpful to other people. We may also have rules about safety and about how to take care of the home.

▼ A village meeting in Baluchistan in West Pakistan. The people have come to talk about how to run the village.

▲ These Algerian women are voting in an election. In an election, each person is given a piece of paper. On the paper, there is a list of people they can vote for. They put an "x" next to the one they choose. The paper is then put into a locked box. The vote is secret.

## Choosing Leaders

In a small group like a family, it is easy to talk about things. A bigger community may have to hold a special meeting. At the meeting, people can decide what has to be done. Communities often choose, or **elect**, leaders. The leaders of a town or city are its **council**. The leaders of a state or country are its **government**. These people are usually elected. The rules they make are the country's laws. Everyone must obey the laws to make sure that the country is well run. If people do not like the laws, they try to elect people who will change them.

## Running a City

Every adult in the city can choose the city council. They can vote for the people who agree with them about how to run the community. Running a city costs a great deal of money. Some people might say they want more schools or hospitals for the city. Others say these would cost too much money. They might say the city needs new roads instead. The city council meets to decide what to do. The **councillors** vote about how to spend the city's money. The councillors each come from a part of the city. They each have one part of the city to look after. The people in that part have chosen them to be on the council.

# Life on a Commune

There is one kind of community where people share many things. It is called a **commune**. A commune is like a large family. Everyone helps to run the commune. They all decide what has to be done and how to do it.

## A Chinese Commune

Chinese communes are very large. Thousands of families may live and work on one People's Commune. There are city communes and farm communes.

The first Chinese communes were set up in 1958 after years of talks and tests on the new system. A commune is run by a **committee** who decide how the land is to be farmed. It is their job to plan the best use of the land. They tell the farmers which crops to grow in which fields and how to improve the soil. Besides rice, the communes grow crops like wheat, corn, and soybeans. Most of the work is still done by hand. Now that the farmers work together, they can grow more food than they need. The commune sells produce to the government in return for money or new seeds, fertilizers, and machines.

All the work on the commune is done by the people who live there. The communes have their own schools, hospitals, and workshops to repair machines. Communes have made it easier for farmers to grow enough food for themselves and their families.

## A Kibbutz in Israel

In Israel, a large farm which works like a commune is called a **kibbutz**. Israel is a dry land. Many kibbutzim are on land that used to be desert. The people had to water, or **irrigate**, the land before they could grow crops. They lived in tents at first. Later on, they built houses. They had to build shelters for their animals, too.

◀ These people live in a village commune in China. Everyone works on the land together. One child here is looking after two younger children so that their parents can work.

The people who started the first kibbutzim wanted to try a new way of life. Many families live together on a kibbutz. Each family has its own home, but all the people work together. The children go to the kibbutz school. Very young children go to the nursery. Their parents share in the work of the kibbutz. When work is over each day, the family can spend some time together.

## Running a Kibbutz

Everyone meets to decide how the kibbutz should be run. The work on a kibbutz is divided up fairly. Everyone gets paid the same.

Some people work on the land. They grow fruit and vegetables. Most of Israel's fruit comes from the kibbutzim. Other people take care of the animals. The animals give them milk, butter, and eggs.

There are household jobs to be done, too. There is a laundry and a kitchen where the food is cooked. All the people eat together in a large dining hall.

▲ Children who live on kibbutzim spend most of the day together. Teachers look after them while their parents are at work.

▼ The people here are working on a kibbutz in Israel. The land has been irrigated. A large field of tomatoes now grows where there was once desert.

# Caring for Others

Most people in a family try to take care of each other. The adults take care of the home and try to make sure that everyone has food and clothes. There are often people in a family who may need extra care. Children are too young to look after themselves. Old or sick people need other people to look after them, too.

## Family Care

In some countries, families have always taken care of the family at home. It is their custom to look after their old or sick people. There is no one else to look after them. These families may live in desert or mountain regions, far away from the towns. In these areas, there are no hospitals or nursery schools. They may see a doctor only once or twice a year when she or he visits their village. The whole family share in the work of caring. Older people may take care of the babies and the children. Then, the parents can carry on working. Someone is always there to care for sick people.

## Community Care

People may want to look after their family, but they may not be able to do so. There may be no one who can stay at home to look after an old or sick person. Sometimes one person in the family may have to give up work to look after a sick relative. The rest of the family has to make sure that they have enough money or food to live on. Sometimes, the country will pay a little money to the person who has the job of taking care of the old or sick relative.

▼ This Japanese family visits their grandfather as often as they can. He does not live with them any more. There is not enough space in their home.

◄ These people live in a home for the elderly. Swimming helps to keep people fit and healthy. It is also fun!

▼ This child is enjoying a game with a ball. The young man is helping the child to hold the ball.

Most countries try to help people who need special care. There are hospitals for sick people. There are nurses and other helpers who visit old people in their homes. There are nurseries for young children. These services cost a lot of money. The family or the whole community may have to pay for these services.

In a few countries, such as Britain and the Netherlands, some older people live in apartments called sheltered housing. They can do most things for themselves. If they need help, they can ring a bell. Someone will come quickly to help them.

People who have no one to care for them may have to live in a hospital or an old people's home. Although people may be cared for by these community services, they still like their families and friends to visit them.

# People Who Help Us

Some men and women are trained to help other people. Their jobs are important in all kinds of communities. These are people like doctors, nurses, and teachers.

## Doctors and Nurses

In a town or city, there are doctors and hospitals. Every family has a doctor. Most of the time the doctor can look after them when they are sick. If they are very sick or have been hurt in an accident, they can go to a hospital. Nurses and doctors will take care of them.

Some people live a long way from the nearest doctor or hospital. In parts of Australia, Canada, and Africa, there is a Flying Doctor service. Doctors are called by radio. They come by plane to treat sick people and to deal with accidents.

In a small village, or on a remote farm, there are no doctors nearby. Once or twice a year, a doctor or a team of **health workers** may visit. The health workers teach people how to keep well.

## Teachers

Children need to learn things which will help them when they grow up. You may go to school for part of the year. If you live in a small village or on a farm, you will need to know how to grow crops and look after animals. You will learn this from the older people around you.

In cities, children go to school for about 11 years. They learn all kinds of things like history, mathematics, science, or art. They may have many teachers while they are at school.

Some children live far away from any school. In parts of Australia, young

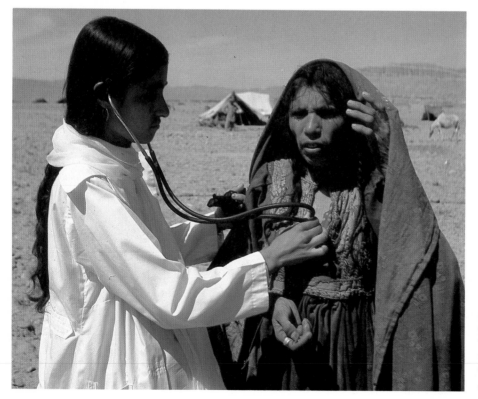

◄ This doctor visits people who live in the desert far away from towns and cities. She may not come to their families more than once or twice a year.

children learn at home. They listen to their teachers on a radio. They can talk to them as well. This is called the School of the Air. When they are about ten years old, they will go to a school in a town. They will live there with the teachers. They come home during the school vacations. Schools like this are called **boarding schools**.

Whether children live in the country or in the town, they all need teachers to help them. Every community needs the help of doctors and nurses.

▶ Libraries are places for people in our community to use. We can go to them to take out books. We can also find out what is going on in the community.

▼ These people in Ghana are learning how to take care of a tractor. The tractor will make it easier for them to farm their land. They may be able to grow more food.

# Sports and Games

People of all ages enjoy sports and games. Many families watch or play sports together. Children often learn how to play different sports at school. They might also join a sports club. Sports and games can be played at some community centers. This is a good way for the whole family to meet people and make friends.

When we play sports, we are also keeping our bodies fit. We need to keep fit so that we do not become sick. People who are unfit catch colds or other diseases more easily. Fit people may live longer, too!

## Team Games

Some sports are team games. Baseball, volleyball, and basketball are team games. They are played in many countries. Soccer is a popular team game all over the world. Many countries take part in the World Cup. It is held every four years. Millions of people can watch the games on television.

Many communities get together to play team games. Towns, villages, and schools often have teams which play against each other. Members of the family who are not playing in the team may go to watch the game.

▼ You can see how much these families are enjoying themselves. They are keeping fit, too. These games are being held in Prague.

▶ Running is a good way of keeping fit and healthy. These families are taking part in a "fun run" in Hyde Park, in London.

## Other Sports

Many children start athletics at school. Some famous athletes were first noticed when they were school children. Often the children are trained by their parents so they can compete in important events.

The biggest athletics event in the world is the Olympic Games. It is held every four years. Each time, it is held in a different country. Men and women from over 150 countries take part in the games. People all over the world watch the games on television.

There are many other sports which families can enjoy together. People of all ages can enjoy swimming, cycling, running, or going for long walks.

Often an adult in a family may have a special skill or interest in a sport like tennis, dancing, or fishing. Then, the children or grandchildren can learn and enjoy that sport, too.

◀ These Korean children are learning karate. It is a popular sport in many parts of the world. No weapons are used. The opponents fight using their legs, heads, hands, and elbows.

# Festivals

**Festivals** are occasions when people enjoy themselves. The people may be happy because of good crops. They may be remembering a special event or person. Some festivals are part of a religion.

Most people have a holiday at festival time. There is a holiday in the United States in November. It is Thanksgiving. This festival has been held ever since people from England went to live in the United States. Those people gave thanks to God for their first harvest. Now, families try to meet to share a special meal. They remember that first Thanksgiving.

## Religious Festivals

Many festivals are part of people's religions. Passover is a Jewish festival. Jews remember the time when Jewish people were slaves. They believe that God helped the people to escape. Passover is also a time when families eat a special meal together.

Muslims hold a festival called Eid Al Fitr. Eid comes at the end of a time called Ramadan. During Ramadan, which lasts for one month, no one may eat in the daytime. At that time, Muslims think about God. They try to be kind to poor or sick people. When Eid comes, prayers are said, and then people visit each other's homes. They give presents of dried fruit and candies. Families share meals with friends.

Diwali is a Hindu and a Sikh festival. It lasts for about five days. Diwali is a festival of lights. It is held in the autumn when there is no moonlight. Little lamps are lit and shine out in the darkness. The Diwali lights show how goodness is stronger than the darkness of evil.

Many places hold a festival just before

◀ This is carnival time in New Orleans, in the United States. At the head of the parade there is a wagon holding the "King of the Butchers." The carnival is called "Mardi Gras." It means Fat Tuesday. It is held before Lent.

Lent begins. Lent is a time when Christians used to stop eating meat. The word **carnival** comes from two Latin words which mean "goodbye to meat." Carnivals are popular in South America and in the Caribbean. The carnival lasts two days and nights. People dance and sing. There are street parades with music.

## New Year

New Year's Day for some parts of the world is on the first of January. For Hindus, the New Year starts in October or November. In the Jewish religion, the New Year starts in September or October.

The Chinese New Year starts in January or February. Celebrations go on for two weeks. People hang lanterns in the trees. There is a special dance in the streets. Sometimes, the dancers wear a lion costume made of paper and bamboo. The old people are given cups of special tea by young people. The young want to show that they care about the old people.

▲ Trinidad and Tobago in the Caribbean have a very big carnival each year. People dress up in colorful costumes and dance in the streets. Bands play loud music. Everyone has a good time.

◄ When Prince Charles married Lady Diana Spencer, everyone had a holiday. People lined the streets to cheer the royal couple. There were parties and fireworks everywhere.

# Sharing with Others

The world we live in is changing fast. We have new kinds of jobs and new ways of living. Families and communities grow and change, too. Our grandparents tell us that things are not the same now as when they were young!

## Feeding the World

There are now over 4 billion people in the world. We all need food, clothing, and shelter.

In Australia, Europe, New Zealand, and North America, most people have enough to eat. Other parts of the world do not have enough food. In these areas, many people live on land where farming is difficult. It is hard for them to grow food. There may be no rain, so no crops can grow. People starve then.

Yet, in other countries, farmers often grow too much food. In Europe, they sometimes produce so much grain that we say there is a "grain mountain." Most people feel this is unfair when there are people in the world who are starving.

Television helps us to understand the problems of others. When we see pictures of starving people, we feel that we want to help them. In 1985, people all over the world learned that people were starving in Ethiopia. A group of musicians called USA for Africa raised millions of dollars. They showed the people of the world how to share with others who need help.

▲ These lorries are taking food to Chad in Africa. People from all over the world have given money to buy the food.

◄ When there is no rain, the crops do not grow. People starve to death or die of thirst. There has been no rain in Ethiopia for a long time. These people have no water. They are waiting to fill their water jars at a place where there is water. They may have walked for days to get here.

## Working Together

Money is not the only thing we can share with other people. We can share what we have learned. If we pass on our knowledge, other people can use it in the way they have to.

When our grandparents were young, there were some diseases which killed thousands of people. Smallpox was one of these diseases. Now, there is no more smallpox in the world. People from many countries worked together to find a cure. Then, they found out how to get rid of the disease.

There are many other diseases in the world. Malaria is one of them. We have to share money and knowledge to find cures for them. We also have to work together so that people in some countries do not starve while other people have too much food.

# All One Family

In one way, all people in the world are like a family. The earth is our home. We expect the people in a family to take care of one another. They all share the home and help to look after it. Many people feel that the world's food and fuel should be shared. There is enough for everyone, but not everyone has enough.

## Different Ways of Life

In a family, we do not expect each person to be the same. We hope they will all be thoughtful and kind to each other, but we know that they are different.

It is the same in the world family. The world is made up of many different communities. They all have their own customs and ways of living. They have different religions and languages. No two communities are really alike.

▶ The earth, seen from space. This is our home in the universe. We are all part of the earth's family.

Often, people are unsure of others who have different ways of life. They may even kill people who have different beliefs or religions. No community can be happy and safe if people do not respect each other. Like members of a family, we can be different, but we can still care for each other.

## War and Peace

People fight for land and wealth. They fight to be more powerful than their enemies, or to defend themselves.

Sometimes, several countries take part in a war. Some wars are smaller. Perhaps two countries will fight each other. If two different groups of people in one country fight each other, that is a **civil war**. The people on each side in a war believe that they are right. They go on fighting until one side is beaten. In all wars, many people are killed or injured.

Since the beginning of this century, the whole world has never been at peace. Wars and hunger cause misery in the world. Wars would not happen if communities could learn to live together as a family. People would no longer starve to death if the human family could learn to share.

# Glossary

**Aborigine:** the name given to the first people to live in Australia. It comes from a Latin word meaning "from the beginning."

**adopt:** to take a child into a family and look after him or her as your own.

**air conditioner:** a machine which controls how warm or cool the air is. Air conditioning makes a building more comfortable to live or work in.

**ancestor:** a relative who lived and died a long time ago.

**arranged marriage:** a marriage that is set up for two people by their parents. The parents find the marriage partners for their children.

**boarding school:** a school where some or all of the children live during the school year.

**carnival:** a festival when there are street parades. There is music, and people dance in the streets.

**celebrate:** to have a party to mark a special event, such as a wedding or a birthday.

**ceremony:** the special way in which important occasions, such as weddings, are carried out.

**chrysalis:** the stage in the life of a butterfly between the caterpillar and the adult butterfly.

**civil:** to do with ordinary life, not religious, legal, or military.

**civil war:** a war where people on both sides come from the same country. They usually fight to see which side will govern the country.

**climate:** the usual weather conditions of a region or country.

**committee:** a group of people who discuss and decide things together.

**commune:** an area of land worked by an organized group of people.

**community:** people who live and work in the same place.

**commuter:** a person who goes to and from work every day by car or public transportation.

**compound:** a group of houses or a village inside its own fence or wall.

**concrete:** a material used for building. It is made from cement, sand, pebbles, and water. When the water dries out, the concrete sets and becomes very hard.

**council:** the group of people who run a town, city, or any other community. They are its leaders.

**councillor:** a man or woman who has been elected as a member of a council.

**cygnet:** a young swan.

**divorce:** to end a marriage between a man and a woman.

**dowry:** the money, land, or goods which the woman brings with her when she marries.

**elect:** to choose or select someone by voting for him or her.

**factory:** a place where goods are made by machine.

**festival:** a happy time when a group of people celebrate. There are many religious festivals, such as Christmas, Diwali, or Passover.

**foster:** a foster parent looks after a child while the child's own parents are unable to do so. The child may go back to live with the parents.

**founder:** a person who starts something.

**government:** a group of people who control a country.

**groom:** to clean or take care of an animal's coat or fur.

**health worker:** a person who teaches other people how to stay well.

**holy:** to do with religion.

**household:** the home and all the things to do with running it. All the people that live in a house.

**instinct:** a way of doing things that animals know without having to learn.

**irrigate:** to bring water to land that has little rain. Crops can grow on irrigated land.

**kibbutz:** a farming community in Israel. Men and women work the land, and all the members of the kibbutz share the profits. Members run schools, hospitals, and nurseries for the children.

**life cycle:** the changes in the life of insects from egg to caterpillar to chrysalis to insect.

**machine:** something that works for us. Machines, such as wheels and drills, help people to do their work more easily.

**mammal:** an animal with a warm body which is usually covered with fur. Mammals give birth to live young which feed on their mother's milk.

**matchmaker:** someone who helps parents to choose a wife or husband for their child.

**material:** anything from which other goods can be made. Stone, wood, and clay are materials.

**neighborhood:** a part of a city or town. A few streets close together may be a neighborhood.

**nomad:** someone who moves from place to place. Nomads do not make their homes in one place.

**polyandry:** having more than one husband at the same time.

**polygamy:** having more than one wife at the same time.

**rabbi:** a leader in the Jewish religion.

**reed:** the stalk of a grass-like plant found by or in the water. It is hollow inside.

**relative:** someone who is part of a family by birth or marriage.

**species:** a group of animals which look alike and can breed with one another. It usually takes two parents of the same species to produce young.

**State:** the nation and its government. Some people in need receive money from the State.

**stilt:** a long pole which acts as a support. Stilts are used to hold a building up above the ground.

**subsistence:** a kind of farming. Subsistence farmers grow food for themselves and their families. They do not grow enough food to sell to others.

**surplus:** an amount of something left over that is more than is needed.

**survive:** to stay alive.

**synagogue:** a building in which Jews meet to pray and in which religion is taught.

**traditional:** describes something which has been handed down from parents to their children for many years.

**tribe:** a large group of related people who live together.

**vote:** to choose a leader. In most countries, people have to be adults before they are allowed to vote.

**workshop:** a room or small place where work is done. Goods are made or repaired in a workshop.

# Index